My name is Lana.

What is your
name? _____

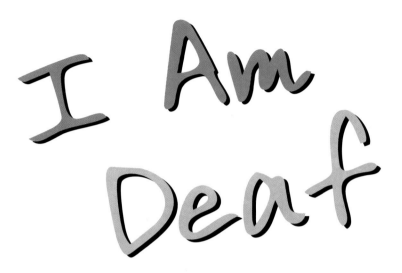

I Am Deaf

Jennifer Moore-Mallinos
Illustrations: Marta Fàbrega

BARRON'S

I CAN'T HEAR VERY WELL

Hi! My name's Lana, I'm ten years old, and I'm deaf. That means that my ears don't work as they should, so I can't hear as well as other people. Some people whose ears are like mine might say that they're hard of hearing or hearing impaired instead of saying that they're deaf. But no matter which way you say it, it means that a person has trouble hearing.

I HAVE FUN ANYWAY!

Being deaf doesn't mean that I can't
do most of the things other kids
of my age can do, and it doesn't mean
that I can't have fun either. I play lots
of sports; I'm even on my school's
volleyball team. I love reading, I have
to make my bed every morning just
like a lot of other kids, and I love
playing computer games too!
The only thing that I can't do
well is to hear.

A REALLY QUIET WORLD

Have you ever wondered what it would be like if you couldn't hear anything? Just think how quiet it would be! Some people are totally deaf, and they cannot hear anything, ever. And then there are those, like myself, who are partially deaf. For us, the world is definitely a lot quieter than it is for most people, but with the help of a hearing aid, the silence can be broken and we can enjoy all kinds of sounds!

A LITTLE DEVICE BEHIND MY EAR

Just like a lot of other kids who
have trouble hearing, I wear
a hearing aid behind my ear.
My hearing aid is so small that
it fits around my ear perfectly and
you can barely see it. My hearing
aid is really good at helping me
hear some sounds, but since
I'm almost totally deaf, I still have
trouble hearing everything even
with its help.

I wear my hearing aid all the time except for swimming or going to bed. At school, whenever I'm in class, my teacher, Mrs. Langley, wears a small microphone around her neck that helps me hear her better. As soon as she starts talking to the class, she turns on the microphone. It doesn't make her voice louder for the other kids, just for me. Somehow the microphone makes my hearing aid work better.
Pretty neat, eh?

HOORAY FOR TECHNOLOGY!

WE CAN ALSO USE OUR HANDS

There are some other kids in my school who are deaf or hard of hearing. Even though we all wear a hearing aid to hear better, sometimes during recess we'll hang out together and talk to each other through sign language.

Do you know what sign language is? Have you ever seen a person use sign language to talk to somebody?

THE BODY LANGUAGE

Sign language is a way for people who are deaf to talk to each other and to other people, like my parents and my brother, who also know sign language. Just like many other things, sign language takes time to learn and it takes a lot of practice too! When we talk in sign language, we say we are "signing." So when I sign, I use my hands to make different shapes that mean certain things. I also use my face and my body to help me communicate how I feel when I am talking. So when I am saying something sad, I make a sad face to help me explain what I am trying to say.

NOW WE HAVE A NEW CLUB!

When the other kids at school first saw us talking to each other through sign language, they stood around and watched. That's when I had a great idea! With Mrs. Langley's help, we started a sign language club. We couldn't believe how many kids wanted to learn. So every morning, the deaf kids and I help Mrs. Langley teach the other kids how to sign. Now during recess, instead of the other kids watching us sign, we all talk together.

LOOKING AT
PEOPLE'S MOUTHS

Not everybody who's deaf or hearing impaired knows sign language. Some can read other people's lips. That means that they can see what a person is saying by the way they move their lips. It takes a long time to learn how to read lips and I still have a lot to learn, but just think how much fun it will be when I get to know what the kids in the playground are saying no matter where I am standing!

USING OUR
EYES INSTEAD

There are a lot of really neat things to help people who are deaf. Some people have special telephones that light up instead of ringing. Since a deaf person wouldn't hear the phone ring, the light tells the person that somebody is calling. Because a deaf person can't hear what the person is saying over the phone, some people have special computers that type out what the person on the phone is saying. The deaf person can then read what is being said on the computer screen. How cool is that?

DOGS NOT ONLY HELP BLIND PEOPLE...

Some deaf people have hearing dogs. The dog's job is to let the person know if they hear something, like if somebody is at the door or if the baby is crying. The dog nudges the owner and then leads him or her to wherever the sound is coming from.

DEAFNESS SHOULD NOT BE AN OBSTACLE

There are many people in the world whose deafness didn't stop them from doing what they wanted to do. Did you know that Thomas Edison, one of America's great inventors, was hearing impaired? And there are actors and actresses on television and in the movies who are deaf!

One day I'm going to do something important too! Maybe I'll become a doctor or a lawyer, or maybe I'll invent something like Thomas Edison did. Mom always says that just because my ears are impaired doesn't mean that the rest of me is impaired too. And that being deaf is no excuse for not trying to be the best I can be.

THE REST OF MY BODY IS OK!

A GREAT FUTURE!

Mom's right! Before I figured it out,
I tried to avoid doing things by saying
that I couldn't because I was deaf. It
took me ten years to understand
that being deaf should not stand
in my way of doing all the things
I want to do, like making friends,
having fun, and dreaming about
the future!

Activities

CARTOON STRIPS

People who use sign language or lip reading to communicate with others need to be very observant (this means to be able to watch something very carefully). Would you like to check how observant you and your friends are? To do that, you'll have to make a cartoon strip!

A cartoon strip is a number of pictures in a row that tell a story. Some use words, some don't. You must plan every picture, so that the entire story makes sense. For that you need to be observant when you are making the cartoon strip, and your friends need to be observant in order to understand what's going on when they read your strip.

Let's create our very own cartoon strip without using words to tell the story.

To get started you will need construction paper or blank paper, pencil, ruler, crayons, and marker pens.

With the help of your ruler, divide your piece of paper into six boxes.

You are now ready to begin drawing your cartoon. Remember, as you move from one box to the next, that your picture should show some kind of progression from one action to another. For example, in the first box you could draw a picture of a monkey on a ladder trying to pick an apple from a tree. In the next box, you could draw the monkey on the ground and the ladder fallen over. This tells the reader that the monkey fell off the ladder to the ground. The following boxes will tell the rest of the story and what happens to the monkey. Be creative, have fun, and don't forget to make your cartoon as funny and colorful as you can.

Show your cartoon to your family and friends and let's see how good they are at knowing what your story is about just from looking at the pictures!

COMMUNICATION CHARADES

Everybody loves charades! It's not only a lot of fun but it's also a great way to learn how to communicate without saying a word.

Let's have a game of charades and only use sign language and lip reading to communicate to the other players.

To get started you will need construction paper, scissors, glue, markers or crayons, stickers (optional), and a timer. Please ask your parents to go to the website www.soundkeepers.com/sign or www.iidc.indiana.edu/cedir/kidsweb/asl.html and download a copy of the sign language alphabet that you will need to play the game. Cut the construction paper into at least 10-15 rectangular pieces (approximately 3 x 5 inches). These are going to be our charade cards. Draw a picture of an animal, person, place, or thing on one side of the charade card. Write the name of your object under each picture. Decorate the other side of the card with colorful designs, polka-dots, or even some fancy stickers. Stack the cards. Now you are ready to play.

Each player takes a turn by taking a charade card from the top of the pile of cards. The person who takes the card will be the Communicator. The Communicator will look at the picture and name on the card, but will not let anybody else see them. The object of the game is to communicate to the other players the picture that is on the card. The Communicator can either use sign language or say the word by moving his or her mouth, but SHOULD NOT make a sound. The players will either have to use their sign language alphabet sheet or read the Communicator's lips in order to guess the answer. You have two minutes to guess correctly! The player who guesses the correct answer gets a point. The player with the most points WINS! Have fun and charade away!

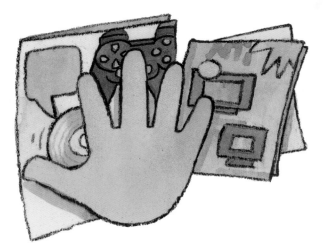

HANDPRINT COLLAGE

Collages are made from many overlapping pictures. Most collages use pictures that reflect a theme. For example, a collage with an animal theme will have many overlapping pictures of different kinds of animals. Let's create a collage that helps us see all the ways we use our ears. For example, we use our ears when we listen to the television and the radio. How many other things can you find?

To begin you will need some construction paper, scissors, glue, old magazines or newspapers, pencil, crayons, and marker pens.

First trace your hand onto a piece of construction paper. Cut out your traced hand. Find pictures in old magazines, newspapers, or your own drawings that you want to include in your collage. Glue the pictures, overlapping them, to your construction paper hand. How many things did you find that you use your ears for?

Now let's make another handprint collage of all the things that a person who is deaf can use, even though they cannot hear. For example, a person who is deaf can still watch television but, instead of listening to the show, they read the writing at the bottom of their screen that tells them what is being said.

Can you think of some other things that people who are deaf can use, even though they are unable to hear? After you have completed both handprint collages, perhaps you will notice that people who are deaf still use many of the same things that people who can hear use, but just in a different way.

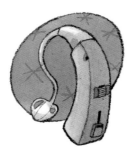

Parent's guide

The purpose of this book is to acknowledge deafness and hearing impairment among children, to describe their environments, and to explore some of the resources available to them. It is hoped that this book will promote a better understanding and acceptance of children who have any level of hearing impairment by eliminating any existing stigma.

Did you know that according to the National Institute on Deafness and Other Communication Disorders, two to three out of every 1,000 children in the United States are born deaf or hard-of-hearing, and nine out of every ten children who are born deaf are born to parents who can hear?

Approximately 28 million Americans have hearing loss. Hearing loss affects roughly 17 in 1,000 children under the age of 18 years. Ten million Americans have suffered irreversible noise-induced hearing loss and 30 million more are exposed to dangerous noise levels every day. Also, only one out of five people who could benefit from a hearing aid actually wears one. This may be due to the stigma, whether perceived or real, attached to those individuals who are hearing impaired.

If you suspect that your child has difficultly hearing, you may want to consider speaking to your family physician about having a formal hearing test in order to determine if hearing loss or impairment is present.

Behaviors that would indicate hearing loss or impairment are difficult to recognize in babies, unless there is some type of obvious irregularity in regard to the ears. However, as your baby grows you may notice some behaviors that could indicate a hearing problem. For example, does your baby respond to your voice or turn toward other sounds within a room? Does your baby respond or get startled by loud noises such as the clapping of your hands? Or when your child reaches the age at which you would expect him to be talking, is he able to pronounce most of the words correctly? Children with hearing loss will often have difficulty saying simple words such as "HI" correctly, mostly because they are unable to hear the word properly when it is being said to them.

Bear in mind that although these characteristics may indicate difficulty with your child's hearing, there could be other reasons why your child is displaying these symptoms. If you have any concerns, you should consult your family physician.

If you discover that your child has a significant hearing deficiency, try not to panic. There are many available treatments, support systems, and technologies that can help your child live a happy and productive life. Exploring the resources within your community in order to determine what is available to you and your child is a good place to start.

I Am Deaf

First edition for the United States and Canada published in 2009 by Barron's Educational Series, Inc.
© Copyright 2008 by Gemser Publications S.L.
El Castell, 38; Teià (08329) Barcelona, Spain (World Rights)
Title of the original in Spanish: *Soy sorda*
Phone: 93 540 13 53
E-mail: info@mercedesros.com
Author: Jennifer Moore-Mallinos
Illustrator: Marta Fàbrega

All inquiries should be addressed to:
Barron's Educational Series, Inc.
250 Wireless Boulevard
Hauppauge, New York 11788
http://www.barronseduc.com

ISBN-13: 978-0-7641-4179-9
ISBN-10: 0-7641-4179-1

Library of Congress Control Number: 2008937340

Printed in China
9 8 7 6 5 4 3 2 1